Charlotte Hussey teaches courses on Breton lais and Old Irish and Arthurian literature at Montreal's Dawson College. She has published *Rue Sainte Famille*, which was shortlisted for the QSPELL poetry award, and a chapbook, *The Head Will Continue to Sing*. Writing a doctorate on the poet H.D. awakened her love of antiquity.

Glossing the Spoils

CHARLOTTE HUSSEY

AWEN
Stroud

First published in 2012 by Awen Publications

This second edition published by Awen Publications 2017
12 Belle Vue Close, Stroud GL5 1HG, England
www.awenpublications.co.uk

Some of these poems have been published in *Eternal Haunted Summer*,
Girlhood Studies, and *Jabberwocky*.

Cover image © 2012 Leicestershire County Council
Coins from the Hallaton Treasure, which is displayed at
Harborough Museum, Market Harborough, England
https://www.leics.gov.uk/harboroughmuseum

ISBN 978-1-906900-52-6

CONTENTS

INTRODUCTION:

CROSSING THE RIVER OF BLOOD

When teaching in James Bay in Northern Quebec, I had a Cree student quietly ask, 'Why are you hungry for our myths and stories? Why don't you go in search of your own?' This sent me on a quest to the UK and on a march through some of the earliest Western European texts – those of the Anglo-Saxons, Celts, French, and Germans.

In most marches, one must ford a river. In a Scottish ballad, Thomas the Rhymer wades up to his knees for forty days and forty nights through the River of Blood to reach the Fairy Queen's enchanted kingdom. An old folk concept, the River of Blood often stood for ancestral memories and forces. In this collection, I am crossing a similar river in order to understand my earliest literary ancestors.

To traverse my own ancestral tributary, I needed, if not a coracle, at least a poetic form with which to paddle across. The Canadian poet P. K. Page has shown me the way through her rediscovery of the glosa. Medieval monks wrote glosses as marginal or interlinear notes to offer word definitions as well as exegetical and critical responses. By the thirteenth century such glosses began to include a category called 'dubia' which allowed questioning and critique. Eventually, from this monastic glossing tradition, a poetic form called the 'glosa' emerged.

To write a glosa, I started with an epigraph composed of four lines from an early medieval text. Interweaving these lines into a new poem, I was able to elaborate, expand, but also sheer off from the epigraph. Academically trained in arts-based enquiry, I was pleased to find that the glosa allowed me to weave ancient passages into my poems and explore intersections between historical, personal, psychological, and mythic states. Sometimes my coracle paddle agitated the build-up of river silt to create a cloudy palimpsest as I searched beneath the Christian overlay for an archaic underwriting. Sometimes I swerved in the Anglo-Saxon sense of 'sweorfan' into completions, corrections, or questions.

Harold Bloom, in *The Anxiety of Influence*, describes this swerve as occurring when the writer veers off from an earlier text in order to critique or correct it. As Bloom reminds us,

> the poet swerves away from his precursor … This appears as a corrective movement in his own poem, which implies that the precursor's poem went accurately up to a certain point, but should have swerved precisely in the direction that the new poem moves.

Thus the exegetical and critical aspects of the glosa made it a wonderful vehicle for swerving!

Some of the notions for my poetic swerves, or critiques, are garnered from my readings of *Landscape and Memory* by Simon Schama, who sees, repeated since the Early Middle Ages, 'the same dismal tale: of land taken, exploited, exhausted; of traditional cultures said to have lived in relation of sacred reverence with the soil displaced by the reckless individualist, the capitalist aggressor'.

Other topics my glosas take up are the modern loss of ritual and myth as ways to contain demonic creation and destruction; Christianity's attempted obliteration of the Pagan and, more personally, a poet's creativity; and, perhaps most importantly, the dimming of poetic ecstasy.

Thus, while crossing the River of Blood, I have listened to, as well as critiqued, those ancestral voices whispering from its turbulence. Doing so has allowed my imagination to mend a break in time, remembering that Page defined 'religion' (re-legere) as to 'read again'. I hope my Cree friend will be pleased; I offer my glosas to him and to you all.

Charlotte Hussey

Time and Again

Out of the curse of his exile, there sprang
ogres and elves and evil phantoms
and the giants too who strove with god
time and again until he gives them their reward.
Beowulf

Did they spring up marked by a curse,
scarring the forehead red,
that of the exile, the outlaw, some old god
trampling the heath, voicing his challenge
like the prolonged scream in the marshes
of something killing something? A bang
(prowler outside my cracked window?)
wakes me startled from an outlandish place,
harried by a beastly hero's harangue.
Out of the curse of his exile, there sprang

the hint of some thing wading closer
through the dark, hungry for flesh;
tight throat, eyes closed, shapes
flood in from a frost-stricken scene,
the fen where it nests, rough and alone.
Weeds choking the mire's bottom,
an enormous head emerges, grimacing,
laughing its gruff, inhuman laughter.
(Am I dreaming up these gruesome
ogres and elves and evil phantoms?)

Monsters banished before Cain
cut down his brother Abel,
they persist. Unable to sleep I wander
past the poster of a psycho TV star
tacked to my daughter's door. He assaults me.
Dots of light in his pupils, odd,
gleaming like hard, barbaric gems;
spots of blood on his face, a criminal's
he killed while working for the crime squad.
And the giants too who strove with god

stared too long into that abyss that stared
back into them and now into him,
our hero driven by his voices to kill.
He's on a mission to purge the city
like a wind cleansing the marshes
of their pestilence, their ill-starred
thistles swollen with seeds.
Vigilante, he is stalking the guilty,
the ice-pick killers in the freight yards,
time and again until he gives them their reward.

Full of Tears

At night there, something uncanny happens:
the water burns. And the mere bottom
has never been sounded
by the sons of men.

Beowulf

Born on the darkest day of the year,
I know how patches of marsh snow,
shadowed in blues, give way
to the raw suck of mud pulling,
pulling off my left rubber boot.
The slick bank steepens: steps
wake the winds to rattle rough
reeds against my face; spits of snow,
the bog pool widens, darkens.
At night there, something uncanny happens.

The water smokes, the air begins
to smoke: two women appear,
as if from some remote within.
Wearing crinkled, white caps,
grey plaid shawls flapping,
they glide, arm and arm. A heron
takes flight as they bend their heads,
conspiring against courage
in the frozen gorse and bracken.
The water burns and the mere bottom

burns icy cold. On the wooden walk-
way skirting the pool, someone
jumps my back, small, not heavy;
chilly hands grab my throat.
We struggle. I throw her off: old
woman, lean, long-legged
as a bird. The others restrain her:
'You have treated her kindly. She is
full of tears. Her mere, so dreaded,
has never been sounded.'

No arms to fall into, just
a surge of dirty water.
I grasp the rail, dig in heels,
scream. Protesting child,
I scream against being your sacrifice,
thrown back into your fen.
Snarling rebellious girl,
I'll scream so as not to be like you,
even if called brazen
by the sons of men.

Tuatha Dé Danann

It was from the north they came;
and in the place they came from they had four cities,
where they fought their battle for learning:
great Falias, shining Gorias, Finias, and rich Murias.
                              Lebor Gabála Érenn

Or was it otherwise they arrived,
not battling the cold and dark
fated heroes wrestle with,
but flying out of the windy light
that comes after a rainsquall?
Swift clouds streaked with flame
wake the eyes to water slightly,
winds humming, the shrubs, the sea
shaken. Seeking freedom without blame,
it was from the north they came

at first like the tiniest out-breath of something
the lips feel shivering over them;
passing through the pale walls of cities
in revolt, their numbers grow, fed
a kind of magic the sun grants
to those steeling themselves for a journey,
a windy light brushing their faces
with its glitter like make-up for a god,
glossing tower and belfry,
and in the place they came from they had four cities,

and a salt wind tunnelling through
a cloud turned molten by the sun.
The cloud tumbles, some loose-skinned,
boneless thing, moulting into shapes
like plunging horses, their seven gaits
written of in lost tracts, listing
their aerial graces and dash,
pages flooded with light, whose leaves
ripple in the wind as they are leaving
where they fought their battle for learning

in those four fabulous cities.
Now in the wind, in the light are flashes,
thrown off the spokes of a wheel,
off a golden cuirass and brooches,
bronze bosses and studs. Their army
hesitates to leap with an airy lightness,
down into time, the wind tearing off
winged ornaments and the fire from their skin
driving them to abandon, like a scavenged carcass,
great Falias, shining Gorias, Finias, and rich Murias.

Lake of the Cauldron

I see a huge man with yellow-red hair
emerge from the lake with the cauldron on his back.
He is a great monstrous man
with an evil thieving look about him.
'Branwen Daughter of Llyr'

A giant within me begins to swim
out of a wilderness lake. Crown
plastered with weeds like a foraging bear,
currents swirling over him,
his paws churn the water like a war,
until his head surfaces into the air.
Water is cascading over the brows,
the eyes, images falling
all around. I too fall there.
I see a huge man with yellow-red hair.

Big-boned knees, vigorous,
striding the bank, he shakes me up,
hungry for the world being born.
Grunting, he rouses the blue glaciers
from their sleep and teaches me not to fear
loud sounds by how he thwacks
his thigh; each slap cracks
like an iceberg shooting into the sea.
I see him, as in a flashback,
emerge from the lake with a cauldron on his back.

Black iron and green brass,
it already smokes, smelling of herbs
as if stolen from an otherworldly feast.
Water beads it. Animals and divinities
decorate it: like a cloudbank swallowing
the sun, a raven spreads its wingspan
over a woman plaiting her dreadlocks.
Long breasts, sweaty belly,
she stirs the cauldron as if it were a pan.
He is a great monstrous man,

but she is quicker to push me into
the boil, against burning metal
searing my stomach. She hacks
shoulder blades, buttocks apart,
scrapes off chunks of flesh,
bones sinking then surging to the rim,
tossed by the churning waters.
He watches her dismember me – wrath,
envy struck away limb by limb –
with an evil thieving look about him.

Green Glass

Later I see a glass tower in the midst of the sea
and see men on the tower
and seek to speak with them
but they never reply.
                    Nennius, *British History and the Welsh Annals*

As if on a psychoanalytic couch,
my words are tossing me about,
sucking me into the departed's wake,
towards a speck on the horizon:
wind kicks spray into the funnel
of a waterspout? Or off to the lee
a whale blows a towering cloud
of glassy bubbles, or a trim schooner
hoists its headsail to apogee?
Later I see a glass tower in the midst of the sea,

mistaking it at first for the spires
of an iceberg calved from ancient snow.
Its grainy coldness seeps in,
leaving me cold and hungry.
The wind shifts: I am bobbed
towards a seven-sided tower
of green glass mirroring my distortions:
tangled kelp, its holdfast gone.
No explanation comes. I feel overpowered
and see men on the tower.

Higher up on the jagged ramparts,
ice-green shadows slide behind glass.
Soldiers commanded into line
by someone with the power of death
in one eye, who raises a heavy eyelid
to petrify me, flesh and bone, condemned
as I am to a luffing dinghy, its jib
slack, my will drained from me.
I can't improvise oars, or a poem
and seek to speak with them.

No deadly eye beam. Indifferent
eyes peer at me through
a billowing updraft of blown snow,
as if the wind I need to tack away
strokes the crown of a giant's head.
I holler. A contrary gust denies
my shouts, freezing them like wings to my sides.
As the vastness, in waves, moves in upon me,
my pleas to these beings intensify,
but they never reply.

Four Corners

Held with poets and plunderers
in this sea-surrounded keep,
I wander its deep halls, dirt floors
strewn with rushes and the herbs of the world,
under which are grease, bones, spittle.
In a niche nested in a wall, the glazed
leaves of a parchment buckle slightly,
as if come alive, to reveal
the raised letters of a phrase:
I am honoured in praise,

a phrase burnished in heavenly gold
that overwrites some faded heresy
inked in cinnabar and cochineal;
the dried blood of an old grammar,
navigation, or lament, injured
by a scraping hand. Deeper, more covered
are faces, grey, overgrown with lichens,
voices that can wake the hills,
cries, sounding birdlike, burred.
Song is heard,

sneaking up from ruination,
where she has crouched for so long;
little, wan woman, ringlets of hair
fall like flax to her calloused heels.
As noon and jet mingle, her lath
body seems cut from a coppice.
She stretches a crooked palm, arm,
genius loci, making new growth
break through the stones of this fastness,
in the Four-Cornered Fortress.

In an underground cell, a solitary
staff planted in the beaten earth
blossoms into a single-stemmed tree;
she hums, bathing my spiralling ears
with tiny, rapid waves,
until the walls of this angular prison
open and, from all directions, bees or spirits
swarm my heart like a storied hive.
Amber tears flood its chambers. I listen,
four its revolutions.

Loathly Lady

You asked neither their cause nor their meaning.
Had you asked, the King would have been made well
and the kingdom made peaceful,
but now there will be battles and killing.
                                    'Peredur Son of Evrawg'

She comes to wake me from a stupor,
the usual sleep. She's hideous,
red face, sagging features,
nostrils flaring like a mule's with every
breath. I can't breathe as she stares
with one speckled eye protruding,
the other sunken and lamp black.
I stand mute in the face of miracles,
large or small. She is screaming:
'*You asked neither their cause nor their meaning.*'

Fists clenched, she's nearly covered
by a blue black mane, twisting
about her like a backlit cloud.
She scowls as her eyes test mine.
The protruding one demands answers;
the sunken obsidian one foretells
what haunts me: a wounded father
grown indifferent to his daughter.
As if I too were deaf, she yells:
'*Had you asked, the King would have been made well.*'

She accuses me of abandoning a king
laid to sleep on a stone slab.
Veiled or winged, a women tends him,
as a red-eared dog laps
long wounds in the king's sides
from which two perpetual
streams of blood and water pour.
How to ask? What is the question
to make this ordeal less painful
and make the kingdom peaceful?

My father's stationed on a stuffed chair,
holding a newspaper come between us.
The dog, not the usual one our family
feeds or grooms, licks him
with a black tongue. The curling and uncurling
tongue, doing and repeating its doings,
the stretch of chin and shaggy throat
free something in me: a howl
not a question, terrible and willing,
but now there will be battles and killing.

Fand, the Fairy Queen

Fand is the tear that covers the eye,
and she is so named for her purity and beauty,
since there is none like her
anywhere in the world.

'The Wasting Sickness of Cú Chulain'

A film of water moistens every eye,
tiny lake with its false bottom
light passes through, threshold awash
between worlds. Little salt sea,
it's where the mind begins to bend
and play with images, magnified
into desires, the hero Cú Chulain's
for Fand, so strong his men
mix him a potion to forget, deny
Fand is the tear that covers the eye.

Fand's first caught in the corner
of his eye, treading across the bay;
its swells, a trick of watery light,
take on the countenance of clouds
rolling in over the abyss.
Eerie like the moon's halo at sea,
pale as dissolving crystals of salt,
she washes away the dust of battle,
the lifelessness from his eyes, quickly,
and she is so named for her purity and beauty.

Cú Chulain's jealous wife
and her fifty maidens with sharpened knives
wait for Fand: a tear trickles
its salt path down his cheek, is gone,
for the living eye is moist, warm,
large, golden. White blur
of her breast, a falcon stoops
into this poem, messenger of fate,
following Fand the world over,
since there is none like her.

Aqua vitae. Spring of vision,
Fand is the tear we all have cried,
cold mornings on the stuffy bus
with its grey faces and its sleepers,
streams of tears and black eyeliner
streaking the cheeks of a girl
I saw there bruised and weeping,
as our wheels spun, and we lurched and swayed,
a crowd of us being hurled
anywhere in the world.

Nine Pipers

They will escape afterwards,
for combat with them
is combat with a shadow.
They will slay and not be slain.
                    'The Destruction of Da Derga's Hostel'

The pipers of that red god Da Derga,
their shrill notes stab at my heart,
waking me at four a.m., lowest point,
emptiest hour when they swarm
from the crevices. Slipping around
the bookcase, they fall downwards
upon me where I lie on my futon,
plunging their lament into my chest,
a dagger twisting inwards.
They will escape afterwards,

after stirring up legions of anger and despair,
like a shadow army to defeat me.
If I breathe, I can outlast them.
If I think of one eye then the other,
closed in fear, wet with sadness,
something breaks the pitch of their mayhem
in this house their road runs through,
forcing a retreat that leaves me
like a bit of their spit-out phlegm,
for combat with them

is combat with a wailing riff,
wild, pulsing through the heart.
Its low drone penetrates
like the buzz of an overlarge fly, circling
the still warm corpse of this night
before dawn, dark as a hedgerow,
and their faces pitted the eerie green
of forgotten gods drowned in a bog.
This bog, with its birls and growling echoes,
is combat with a shadow,

17

their shadows and those of Da Derga.
I see him at dawn moving behind
the backyard fence, hood up
like a dog walker, red of his coat
bleeding through the weathered slats,
martial, awakening colour like memory's stain
stuttering through a breech in time.
The backyard waits – slippery, packed-down snow –
for his pipers' return; their harsh campaign.
They will slay and not be slain.

Against Elf-Shot

I stand under linden, under the bright shield
where those mighty women consult their powers
and they send screaming spears;
I will send them back another one.

                    'Wid Faerstice'

Linder, to soothe just about anyone:
the suddenly tired, the accident prone,
the criminal on the eve of his trial,
even the crying child. In her sleep,
she stirs fitfully with some phantom
thing abroad. Echoes across the fields,
pipes and reeds, tolling bells
haunt me under this linden tree,
as if it were rooted on a battlefield.
I stand under linden, under the bright shield,

listening to these women's pounding steps,
the hems of their gowns singed with fire,
the tough skin of their heels scraping
the edges of sleep, as they circle
the slippery mountaintop, the smooth
barrow. Unstoppable their willpower.
There's no appeal they will listen to.
Horses readied to leap hedges,
they seize their spears; the wind still lours
where those mighty women consult their powers.

Surly riders entering the bone-house
like lice on a head, they jump and attack.
Tiny spears the eyes cannot blink
away speed through the night
into the poorly laced-together places –
hunger, loneliness, and fear –
bunched seams ripped through.
Their hunch: to force entry into a bed
of lacks, all that spits and leers,
and they send screaming spears.

Out, out as I emerge from sleep.
Leap out of me, poisonous foam.
Go back home to your height,
to where these disease-shooters dwell.
Break your point on piled stones.
Wash off your venom in the hilltop
stream. Rust iron in its millrace.
These mighty women have lied to you
that, O Spear, I can be overcome –
I will send them back another one.

Naked

The Giant will climb on the Dragon,
throw off all his clothes
and then ride upon it naked.
The Dragon will rear the Giant up into the air.
        Geoffrey of Monmouth, *History of the Kings of Britain*

The seventy-foot giant cut out of chalk
on the Cerne Abbas downs is shaped
from the lines of a mountain or plain. Grand,
naked like them, he raises a knotted
cudgel over his head, lips grimaced.
He's defending his turf, toughened
nipples like second eyes; roused
cock sticks out from his thighs,
a taunting tongue, a blackthorn. Maddened,
the Giant will climb on the Dragon.

Or is the nude one Georgia O'Keeffe
who paints with those same large, clarifying
strokes people with big passions use
to coax a dragon from a buff hill?
Unclothing it except for the scruffy cedars,
she curves her lines until the hill's nose,
a grey cliff-chimney, and its crenulated,
Jurassic neck heave out of the mesa.
She learns to do this when asked to pose,
throw off all her clothes

for her husband Stieglitz who photographs her:
the raised tendons of her neck twisting
from the collarbone's bas-relief,
mountain-ridges out of the land,
breasts like sloping sand hills,
hipbones, their gullies shaded.
Caught painting in the raw, she shakes
her brush at her peeking nieces like a shillelagh,
to evoke a dragon, horned, crested,
and then ride upon it naked.

Kandinsky, her inspiration, likened
the colour wheel to a serpent biting its tail,
balancing hot and cool, light and dark.
Rocks slipping, no path,
O'Keeffe scrambles up the flint butte
to see for miles the serpent there,
its folds the water-starved badlands,
blood reds, purples, the greens
of her mesa. Loosed from his pebbly lair,
the Dragon will rear the Giant up into the air.

Daemon Lover

Many times too when I am sitting alone,
he talks with me without becoming visible,
and when he comes to see me in this way,
he often makes love with me.
      Geoffrey of Monmouth, *History of the Kings of Britain*

Alone in my small yellow room,
I lie on my futon, not quite a nun
like Merlin's soon forgotten mother.
Nameless queen kept or keeping
to her cell, she sought sanctuary from love's
burning stake, its ashen throne.
The moonlight through the open casement
bathed the froth of her gown as the silvered
leaves in the garden stirred on their own.
Many times too when I am sitting alone,

the rustle of leaves in the night garden,
the perfumes of hawthorn and purple lilac
make me call out to him as she did
out of a branching maze of dreams,
forking river that flows into the heart
through the back, cushioned with its invisible
wings, petals, leafy feathers.
Uncurling, softly adorning the air,
they announce his approach, so pleasurable.
He talks with me without becoming visible,

save for once or twice when he,
taking off a sawtoothed crown,
flies from his shaded perch in the maple,
wings lustrous as the undersides of its leaves
that are brushing the raised window.
It is his voice that enters straightaway,
a breeze against my thin frock
just before the images form
of lips that might be cruel, some say,
and when he comes to see me in this way

it is the voice of someone watching
beside me, over me, in me
whispering: 'You are a beautiful woman,'
a voice mesmeric as moonlight forcing
buds vining up the green trellis
to burst and float towards ecstasy,
moist-petalled, huge and white.
It is his voice that says, 'Expect
nothing.' Speaking this way, as to a lady,
he often makes love to me.

Words

He'll need
a way
with words
indeed.

                    Robert de Boron, *Merlin*

Boron would write his own gospel
like a fifth Evangelist, rivalling
the good tidings, the telling parables
of Matthew, Mark, Luke, and John,
but the only itinerant miracle worker
he can find is that local half-breed
Merlin, whose father's a spirit of air,
loosed, rushing not around,
but through our dreams until they are freed.
He'll need

to pen his holy writ with care,
for the Pope's burning Cathars for less.
Once a princess on a high seat,
Merlin's mother must now descend
from a family bankrupted by suicides.
She'll be stoned, or burnt at the stake midday,
for fancying an Annunciation Angel
lookalike who rouses her passions,
impregnates her imaginings led astray.
A way

must be found for Boron's words
to keep the religious meek and mild.
But what of Ezekiel granting a face
to the Four Directions and their Winds:
Eagle, Lion, Bull, and Man,
whirlwinds I hear blustering downwards,
over the bony rafters like the inrush
of an ardent spirit coursing
the squall line of this March blizzard?
With words

stilled, my tongue's like one stuck
to an icy, metal fence. Beyond
the whiteout, I sense Merlin's father,
the one Boron calls Hequibedes,
or his smell: pines and sea wrack.
Snow smokes like raw incense, eddied
off the drifted garden, that my hands
reach through, traces of what
he is and isn't. Not words to misread,
indeed.

The Singers

You have never heard such singing as theirs
but when their song is most pleasant to you
a great moaning and groaning comes
towards you through the valley.
            'Owein, or the Countess of the Fountain'

After I lose you, grief,
fasting, prayer, cloistered
in a tiny, rented room
meditating six hours a day,
up from my pelvis, navel, heart
a flock of white birds tears
open my inward gaze, exploding
out of my throbbing skull,
a storm clearing the air.
You have never heard such singing as theirs.

Hundreds of voices carol
to the tinkling of silver necklets, chaining
the flock together to draw something
across the sky, or out of me:
a liquid gold, a concentrated
fire oozes, pouring through
the tingling hole they've pierced
between my eyes, dense gold,
my body its melancholic residue.
But when their song is most pleasing to you,

as I imagine you, imagine holding you,
their necklets, yoked together
to empty me to death,
rattle out a jarring note.
Their wings rush above its pulse
that rasps at my eardrum,
too small to hear the birds for long;
too alone, too afraid. Cloud shadows,
they depart, leaving me stunned.
A great moaning and groaning comes

like the keening after lost kin,
played on a crude pipe, with sympathies
for lightning and muted thunder.
I hear weeping inside, outside, as drops
of water blacken a stone, rain
stone, storm stone an off-key
crow scratches at and pecks.
With my muddy feet and my knapsack
full of lost chances, I will journey
towards you through the valley.

Silver Branch

The branch springs from Bran's hand
so that it is in the woman's hand,
for there is not enough strength
in Bran's hand to hold it.
                    'The Voyage of Bran, Son of Febal'

I cut a branch from a crab apple
deep in the wood, a silver branch,
and dream all night of how to dress it:
silken ribbons of purple and blue,
seven hawk bells dangling in a row.
I am quickly made to understand
the branch possesses a potency all its own,
calling, called to those it chooses
like the silver one from fairyland;
the branch springs from Bran's hand.

Bran has dreams too. Waking,
he finds a silver branch in blossom,
a woman entering his locked fort.
She sings of a cultivated island: music
in the air, fragrant with vines and fruit,
sky-blue horses cantering the sands,
and joyful women awaiting him.
Bran is called to go; the silver branch
leaps like a lure from his hand,
so that it is in the woman's hand.

Mine falls prey to other hands,
my own in this age of scientific fact.
I forget my branch on a library shelf.
Dust from the streets covers it,
clouding my desires, leaving me
to starve in spite of the feasting, the wealth,
deaf to the dream-maker's approach:
her branch cannot pull me out of time,
her songs do not go on at length,
for there is not enough strength

in my hands to grasp this gift,
this flowering branch and my breath, wind
through one of its bells. I linger on
among sceptics in barren rooms,
humouring their questions and doubts,
dissecting nothing but what is minute,
nothing compared to a silver branch,
the tones and half-tones of its bells
brimming over a level sea, the delight
in Bran's hand to hold it.

Wyvern

Merlin sits still for a long time,
as though he is struggling greatly with a dream.
Those that see it with their own eyes
say he often twists as if he is a worm.
                                    Layamon, *Brut*

Merlin, his rapt figure's chiselled
on the corbel table of this Norman church,
as if dropped into the coils of a dream,
seeking a prophecy, or his father.
His blank, sandstone eyes, worn
of their painted pupils by the longtime
rain, stare like those of the dragon,
wyvern, or worm that juts from the eaves
that dreams of a prediluvian springtime.
Merlin sits still for a long time,

he, the Old Man of the Forest, encircled
by a bestiary carved on the outside
parish church walls: wolf,
crow, the hunt of dog and darting hare;
the fair with its oxen, pig, and lamb;
the fishmonger's catch laid out by the stream –
where a Roma leads a muzzled bear,
and a dancer, or wrestler, throws ursine
arms around a man and screams,
as though he is struggling greatly with a dream,

a dream that smells musty and of mice,
where a tonsured priest holds up
a scourge and aspergillum, guiding
all inside. One leaden window
set into the airless nave pours
hazy light down from the skies.
Dust motes like the fallen descend
upon stones as an ashen-faced
penitent paces and beats at his thighs.
Those that see it with their own eyes

see something older than sin:
a dragon flying over the roof arch,
over the gravestones leaned into the rain,
the heaped bouquets, their stems and browned
petals culled from the newly dead.
Its horns rake at the clouds, its firm
belly, yellow as lightning, writhes,
like Merlin waking at last from his dream.
When he does, people say he squirms,
say he often twists as if he is a worm.

Raven Knowledge

Should my tongue be loosened by greed, or lightness,
Should it be puffed up by vanity – then my familiar spirit –
that being by whom I know what I know
would withdraw his inspiration from my breath.
                    Wace, *Roman de Brut*

Merlin evokes what Emily Brontë
hungers for, his daemon a thing of breath,
or riding his breath like a bird a thermal.
Some say it is his incubus father,
roving like a crow or raven, who knows
what the cawing means, the raw otherness
of their bach, bach, or the softer err, err
humming to or through Merlin
as he wanders the snowy wilderness.
'*Should my tongue be loosened by greed, or lightness,*

he would leave my mouth empty,'
Merlin says when the King demands
to know his future. With a mind willed
from treetop to treetop, Merlin sees only
battle carnage and a wayward queen.
His daemon forbids telling the secrets
of that gulf of gorging ravens,
regurgitating a history that can easily
roar over the tongue of any prophet.
'*Should it be puffed up by vanity – then my familiar spirit*

will still my tongue.' Brontë's familiar
is a thing not of breath, eddying
over the tongue, but of the winds
buffeting the house as she secretly writes
late at night on her lap desk.
Candles flutter in the rattling windows,
announcing the wanderer who squalls,
harrying the moor, stopping her heart.
Father Nature, or a giant of the frost and snow?
'*That being by whom I know what I know,*

she tells herself. Her father a preacher
not an incubus, she hears its daemon-moan
as it stoops over the eaves, the manse,
the snow-wreathed graveyard,
suffocating her words; her abyss
not the blasts of history, but the death
wish. Merlin, his breathy auguries dying
in and out, warns, 'My familiar, if I
take liberties with his dark truths,
would withdraw his inspiration from my breath.'

Devil May Care

There is one among us who is able
to take on the appearance of a man
and make a woman conceive
but he has to do it as discreetly as possible.
                                    The Prose Merlin

'Although you humans have painted us
with goose feet, a gnarled tail,
leering eyes on our buttocks, and a member
like a mule's, thick and muscular as an arm,
we are more like a breeze stirring the clover
that makes an unbuttoned chemise tremble,
brushing the breasts of a lone woman in a field,
her limbs agitated as if by our touch.
If only our forms were more solid.
There is one among us who is able

to condense, from the night air and its vapours,
a body for himself, at first female,
so as to sleep with a male, some chaste youth
tingling again from a wet dream,
whose white spume is easy to cup
and carry away bare-handed,
like the cream we steal from a dairy pail.
Because our seed is but chilled dew
strewn on the grass, our colleague must then plan
to take on the appearance of a man.'

'He puts on a pleasing face and big
body parts to fill up
my secret places,' a woman once
told her inquisitor. 'His parts are bigger
than human and soft as cotton wool,
or flax densely packed to deceive.
Like the stuffing for my bed quilt,
he slides against me. Ones like him
apply their organs without leave
and make a woman conceive.'

'But how', a metaphysical voyeur
might ask, 'does he carry the youth's
vis vitalis around without
spilling some? Smeared on milkweed leaves
picked in a marsh on St John's Eve,
or in the hollow stem of dock, or bramble?
Is he simply doing his devilish duty
for god and country?' 'No, he enjoys
it as much as her. Never a grumble,
but he has to do it as discreetly as possible.'

Make Over

'My Lord, rub your hands and face
with this herb.' The King does so
and unmistakably takes on
the appearance of the Duke.

The Prose Merlin

King Uther Pendragon lusts
after his duke's wife, the Fair Igraine.
Sighing, pining, turning pale,
refusing all food, he's suicidal.
His men scour forest and shore
for Merlin's gathering places
to find him harvesting his fresh
leaves, seeds, and dug-up roots,
some thick as a thumb, some like lace.
'My Lord, rub your hands and face

with this salve of henbane and lard,'
Merlin says, brought back reluctantly
to the castle from a sandy waterside, crowded
with colonies of bell-shaped blossoms.
The greyish, sticky wool of their leaves
rubbed against bared arm or elbow
can cause giddiness or stupor.
'Daub this unguent on yourself, My Lord.
Your body will melt like tallow
with this herb.' The King does so,

with fumbling hands, smearing it
on temples and cheeks. He begins to pace,
as if his imaginings were jostled about
by black bile ascending to the brain.
Misty with sweat, his features blur,
a mass of flesh. Small convulsions
shake his nose and bushy brows
as bones float and bend.
His face quiets its agitation
and unmistakably takes on

the Duke's likeness. No plastic surgeon's
cheek implants or hairline cuts
could form it better. As Uther
lies with Igraine, she beholds her husband's
narrower nose, squared jawline,
and its manly cleft. Their look doesn't spook
her ladies-in-waiting. But those dilated eyes,
hungering after her, another man's wife,
alter slightly, but without rebuke,
the appearance of the Duke.

Trolls

Watch out for trolls
on the road! One or other
of my troll keepers will
deprive you of joy!
                    Wolfram von Eschenbach, *Parzival*

The Old High German 'trollen'
means 'running with small steps',
rustling the undergrowth of a forest,
where a knight, mounted on a monumental,
high-stepping horse, hacks
far from his thick-walled stronghold.
The clop of the shod hooves over shale
drowns out the drier sounds
of leaves being crushed by feet like a mole's.
Watch out for trolls!

As if long fingers were dropping coins,
there's a dull ringing on the barren ledges,
where a treasure trove, brought out to air,
can appear but a pile of dirt.
Dusty pebbles, loosened by something,
suddenly spill as if from a coffer,
their slurred clatter growing fainter,
further down in the leaf-fall,
near trees that sough and whisper
on the road. One or other

of the winds, camped on the muddy slope,
lends its gritty force for a time
to something huffing like a feral hound
through a nose bigger than human;
its nostrils flare as it leaps rotting
logs, crashing its way downhill
towards the knight who's expecting a leathery-
winged, warty-skinned, bony-
snouted devil! 'Thinking ill
of my troll keepers will

defeat you,' the Lady had warned.
The knight, lifting his fluted, iron
visor with its narrow sights,
stares out of the menacing helm.
His steely eyes fix on some distant
vanishing point: a crusading convoy
to join, another holocaust to start,
or a melancholic witch to burn.
'Thoughts about whom next to destroy
deprive you of joy.'

Matter

And he sees the shield at his neck
great and black and ghastly at its centre.
He sees the dragon's head throwing out
fire and flame with a terrible force.
                                          Perlesvaus

In Welsh bogs and English fens,
war gear is ruined then drowned.
A wolf-embossed sword, bent;
a boar, bulging amber eyes
cresting a helmet, sheered off,
smashed; the raven shield decked
with raw red stones, defaced.
They harbour vengeful spirits, beaten,
sacrificed to the gods and their cromlechs.
And he sees the shield at his neck

as they collide. Pounded from meteoric
metals on an anvil's tempered horn,
its dragon-faced boss spits
an acrid, scalding mist. Perceval
stabs into the flame-thrower's gullet
to kill the battle furore
of his enemy. Helms, twisting
torcs rattling under the sun,
they clash and clash again; their clamour,
great and black and ghastly at its centre,

awakens the banshee to glide
her wolfhounds over the moor,
their phosphorous eyes, their fangs
sharp as the cold, clanging steel
Perceval drives through the toothed
flange of the dragon shield, routing
its magic. He thrusts, thrusts
into its copper throat where black,
smoking blood begins to spout.
He sees the dragon's head throwing out

41

its last volley, the enemy's shield
clattering to stony ground. Its matter
the same imploding cyclone of atoms
that flash-burns and blows apart
a Hiroshima. Encased now in fat
metals, a gadget without remorse
self-destructs. Nothing's left to sacrifice,
just a scar burning across the land,
where blast winds run their course,
fire and flame with a terrible force.

Brigit

And one side of her face is ugly,
but the other side is very comely.
And the meaning of her name
is Breo-saighit, a fiery arrow.

                    Lebor Gabála Érenn

Cool air, misty breath,
a virgin king is led through a forest
to a stream and seated amid ferns,
facing a big-shouldered woman
in a rough cape, its collar decorated
with the ribs of something large. From this gravelly
bank, she plunges a bronze cup
into the spring overflow, offering him
a solemn drink, pure yet chilly.
And one side of her face is ugly.

Or is it her whole face? Her skin's
furrowed and black as burnt bark,
her lips cracked, her lidless eyes
stare unflinching into the king's.
Waving her arms like raptorial wings,
she takes him under her cape, dirty,
run through with burrs and thorns.
Hearing only the boiling stream, the king's
dragged to the bottom swiftly,
but the other side is very comely,

the other bank, the returning swans,
her other face? She is ripping off
the hag's mask, throwing it over
her freckled, milky shoulder.
Touched by sunlight, her golden hair
swings free, her crown's aflame.
The king buries himself in her soft,
full breasts. Held fast
in her embrace, his sovereignty's proclaimed.
And the meaning of her name?

Ask her own Abbess of Kildare
who by 1132 C.E.
dresses in a wimple and won't let
any man dally under her habit,
until her thorn hedge is penetrated
by a hooligan king who throws
her on a sagging straw pallet,
breaks her like the branch that fans her fire,
for she, a shaft of spring willow,
is Breo-saighit, a fiery arrow.

Fisher King

And so they lead him to the chamber
where the Fisher King lies
which seems to be strewn
with grass and flowers.

Perlesvaus

The Fisher King lies in a room
smelling of the river. Its reed grass and sedges
covering the floor are strewn
with wild flowers: cowslips and lavender spikes,
and, of course, clover to avoid madness.
Windows of green glass shower
down light as everything wavers
as if underwater. Is the Fisher hale,
or grey as a dying river elder?
And so they lead him to the chamber,

another promising hero to see this king
who leans against pillows groaning
from a wound in the thigh, or groin.
A river slides through it, brown
with the sunken foliage of a Viet Nam
jungle; he watches it explode into a floodway
sucking his recruits suddenly from shore
into a kill of snakes and seepage, all
the bamboo groves napalmed in the melee.
Where the Fisher King lies

in his carved oak and curtained bed,
his thoughts drift to last summer,
burying his buddy in a family plot.
A convoy of ageing motorcycle knights
comes to attention, as a cannon volleys
its salute over a humid field, its platoons
of daisies, cowslips, and clover.
Sulphur and singed petals smudge
the air, incense for the dead. This afternoon,
which seems to be strewn

around him like pollen grains on a tomb,
he honours the hero's departure with a whisky,
begins again to write a few
lines of seduction, or plans for escape
to a woman confused for letting him
pour his deluge into her, overpowering
her dream of a fountain where tulips
nod their tended heads; she knows
he lies alone in his river-washed tower,
with grass and flowers.

Fortuna

In memory of Dr Jacqueline Kirk (1968–2008)

With her white hands she whirls round a wheel
as if she might suddenly upset it completely;
the rim is red gold set with rare royal stones,
arrayed with richness and rubies aplenty.
                              Alliterative *Morte Arthure*

Did you dream as King Arthur did
before his final battle that Fortuna
would suddenly throw you down too?
August 13, that unluckiest of days,
you are travelling a bone-jarring road,
dust blowing over the windshield
of your white truck, on a mission
from Gardez to Kabul. The rocky ground,
even the midday sun, is concealed.
With her white hands she whirls round a wheel,

or wheels bumping into potholes,
as you enter a dun-coloured village,
mud homes, scrubby vineyards.
Here Fortuna, eyes nearly blinded
by the hanks of her greasy hair, hides
behind an orchard wall, deadly
its fruit of Kalashnikovs poised
amid the grapevines and pomegranates.
Your truck careens, strafed repeatedly,
as if she might upset it completely.

Flashes of fire; the villagers flee
the gunmen. Preferring anonymity,
a doctor, travelling that scarred road,
takes note: everybody in the shredded
vehicle looks like they are curled up,
in their torn seats together, alone.
Rolling up her bloody sleeves,
Fortuna spins her hissing wheel.

A line, beginning and end unknown,
the rim is red gold set with rare royal stones.

In this nearly treeless land, your coffin
is plain and narrow. Bleached cotton
swathes you like an angelic burka.
If only Brigit, prophesying at her loom,
could raddle threads steeped in cloudberry,
dandelion root, and lichen and deftly
bind you back into a becoming cloth,
a brocade that can never tangle
with Fortuna's fickle spindle, so treacherously
arrayed with richness and rubies aplenty.

The Questing Beast

The beast goes to the well and drinks,
and the noise is in the beast's belly
like the questing of thirty coupled hounds,
but all the while the beast drinks.
Thomas Malory, Le Morte d'Arthur

The earth is spinning faster, faster.
Pick-ups that once hauled melons
bristle with guns and flashed V-signs.
Volcanoes wake spewing ash.
Financial fault lines strain and slip
as the richest one per cent hoodwinks
the rest. My laptop streams an oasis,
where a rough beast, possibly me,
stands on the greenstone brink.
The beast goes to the well and drinks.

Eye of the earth sunken in sand,
the well reflects back the ancient
Babylonian sky, its beasts spiralling
out of the dark: solar calf,
barbed dragon, astral goat-men
come dancing in an unearthly
dream. We wobble on wine-spilled legs,
hair streaming in a widening spin.
A deep howl assails us suddenly,
and the noise is in the beast's belly.

Half-lion, half-woman,
lightning flaming from her forearms,
breast stones and lapis anklets,
she raises a mace drenched in blood
as the booming voice of drum or cannon
throws us face down on the ground.
She carries a spell in her mouth
to place unending tears in our eyes,
an angry lament in our heart that sounds
like the questing of thirty coupled hounds,

desert packs that clamour at full cry
following her leonine tracks
across wastes scorched by her breath.
Unseen, sealed from us except in dreams,
she destroys, builds up, tears down.
To quell this blood-lusting sphinx,
I raise my nose from the ground,
my supplicating lips from the dust,
as the stars in the well dwindle and sink,
but all the while the beast drinks.

Tree

For H.D.

On the bank of the river,
he sees a tall tree:
from roots to crown one half is aflame
and the other green with leaves.

'Peredur Son of Evrawg'

She passes through a charred wall,
door blown off, its skeletal
frame leaning inwards. The drone
of the bombing squad begins to fade
as an eerie music like wind through the ribs
of something large grows louder,
rising over the rubble, stirring her
to cry and laugh and wish to sleep,
not knowing whether, like a dreamer
on the bank of the river,

she is there or not. For this music
makes her feel invisible, as if
ascending its ladder of rippling notes,
away from all plague and havoc,
or is she climbing an arched bridge
through mists, vaulted steeply
over brown water? Or, in a crowd,
is she following a man who talks to himself
while entering a city square? Only
he sees a tall tree

as if it were a sceptre raised
to still the trampling feet of the crowd.
Or is he the tree's guardian seated
on a low mound like a young lord,
pointing to the paths leading from it,
from this May tree with its many names:
Lady of the Snows, Primavera,
Gala, Melba, Beauty of Stoke,

51

Red Sleeves, Scarlet Flame?
From roots to crown one half is aflame,

has been aflame, this half-scorched,
stricken tree, come so near
like a maimed immortal bearing the seal
of death, as if to prepare for a burial.
She bows and weeps, bows and weeps
to see how its other half cleaves
to life: sinewy branches, plump red buds
widening into white petals, and the tree –
one half is dead – so she believes –
and the other green with leaves.

Ogress

In a month and a fortnight,
this woman will conceive
and the boy that she bears at that time
will be a fully armed warrior.

                    'Branwen Daughter of Llyr'

Her name is Kymidei Kymeinvoll,
a naked, black-faced ogress,
who often importunes gentlemen
straying too deep into the forest.
Urging them on with her noisy wooing
until their ears throb with fright,
Kymidei squats akimbo in the dirt
on brawny, rough knees, the earth
of her rugged cave, quaking with delight.
In a month and a fortnight,

she gives birth to a burly lad
who breaks her water with a bronze sword
and bounds off into the fray.
Kicked out of Ireland, she wades to Britain
but, like the painter Emily Carr,
forgoes its civilising reprieve.
Kymidei gradually dwindles away
into a picturesque garden.
Carr, on the other hand, decides to leave.
This woman will conceive

her own colossus in a rain forest
in a tangle of eight-foot nettles,
rank, prickling forehead and ears.
Dzunukwa, a carved potlatch ogress,
startles her: black brows jutting,
pursed red lips primed
to scream a numbing 'Hu! Hu!'
Her grizzly arms reach to hug
some boy out past his playtime,
and the boy that she bears at that time,

bears away in her cedar basket,
will escape Dzunukwa when she gets drowsy,
as Carr will escape the nettle thicket,
but not without stumbling over
a rotten log. As its bark gives way,
a wasp whirs, wings a copper
blur, out of its papery nest.
Fuelled on fresh nettle juice,
brandishing its barbed lance at her
will be a fully armed warrior.

Immram

Plenteous are the wonders
upon the blue wave's kingdom;
swift is the sailing
when Maelduin makes his voyage.
            The Voyage of Maelduin

'What drove your people to sail west?'
a Cree student asks in our Arctic trailer,
the temperature hovering at minus fifty outside.
'Not hard,' a bard of old would say.
'It's the open-ended curve of our art
lifting our boat like a wave, its rowers
and bailers, from off a windy headland
with its cliff-castle into the Great Sea.
It is the restless art of the wanderer.'
Plenteous are the wonders

to lure him offshore: celestial music
shaken from a branch by a stranger,
or the poetry of a trickster god,
rolling his chariot over the flood.
His promise: beyond the sallow fog
lies an isle without grief, or gruesome
death, a place of tilled land
and white cliffs warmed by the sun.
Soon monks begin falling like flotsam,
upon the blue wave's kingdom,

throwing themselves to the fierce, green
tide like criminals cast off
in hide-covered boats without rudder,
or oars. Seeking penitence or the truth,
they remember what their new god
told Abraham: 'Go forth, leaving
your native land and your father's house,
to the land I shall show you.'
Winds brawling, a whale spouting,
swift is the sailing

in the old yarns of the seafarers, older
than the standing stones they navigated by,
trading their ingots of copper and tin,
brokering in time and space to the oars'
creak and splash, catch and drive.
Watching the sea swallow the ridges,
the green slopes, the gentle hills,
the crew bursts into a shanty – bravado
overriding lament – sculling from their moorage,
when Maelduin makes his voyage.

NOTES AND ACKNOWLEDGEMENTS

Poetic licence (fairy glamour) occurred with a few of the epigraphs: their verbs were changed to the present tense and their verbiage compressed, to achieve a more seamless flow between ancient and modern.

p. vii. P. K. Page, quoted in Allan Brown, Review of *Hologram: A Book of Glosas* by P. K. Page, *Antigonish Review*, 2010.

p. viii. Harold Bloom, *The Anxiety of Influence: A Theory of Poetry*, Oxford University Press, New York, 1973, p. 14.

p. viii. Simon Schama, *Landscape and Memory*, Vintage Books, New York, 1995, p. 13.

p. 1. *Beowulf*, trans. Seamus Heaney, W. W. Norton, New York, 2000, p. 9. Does the hero become the monster he fights?

p. 3. *Beowulf*, p. 95. The devouring creatrices Nerthus and Ceridwen are conflated here with Grendel's mother.

p. 5. *Gods and Fighting Men: The Story of the Tuatha De Danaan and of the Fianna of Ireland*, trans. Lady Augusta Gregory, Forgotten Books, London, 2007, p. 13. The godlike Tuatha Dé Danann were allegedly the fifth wave of invaders to conquer Ireland.

p. 7. 'Branwen Daughter of Llyr', in *The Mabinogion*, trans. Jeffrey Gantz, Penguin, London, 1976, p. 72. The old tales often prefer a nadir, instead of a climax, as with this plunge into the Gundestrup Cauldron.

p. 9. Nennius, *British History and the Welsh Annals*, ed. John Morris, Phillimore, London, 1980, p. 20. A ninth-century monk, Nennius, supposedly composed this history.

p. 11. 'Preiddeu Annwn: The Spoils of Annwn', trans. Sarah Higley, Camelot Project, University of Rochester. Adventurers to the Welsh otherworld of Annwn go in search of spoils and inspiration.

p. 13. 'Peredur Son of Evrawg', in *The Mabinogion*, p. 249. The Loathly Lady goads Peredur for disastrously failing to ask the Noble Question.

p. 15. 'The Wasting Sickness of Cú Chulain', in *Early Irish Myths and Sagas*, trans. Jeffrey Gantz, Penguin, London, 1981, p. 160. The Irish bards' likening a fairy woman to a fragile teardrop shows profound understanding of our eyes' wish-fulfilling sorcery.

p. 17. 'The Destruction of Da Derga's Hostel', in *Early Irish Myths and Sagas*, p. 82. The nine sidhe pipers are supernatural warriors appearing during the resurgence of Halloween chaos overtaking the Red God Da Derga's Hostel.

p. 19. 'Wid Faerstice', trans. Stephen O. Glosecki, in *Shamanism and Old Irish Poetry*, Garland, London, 1989, pp. 110–11. This Anglo-Saxon 'Charm Against a Stitch' was used to repel Valkyrie-like disease-shooters.

p. 21. Geoffrey of Monmouth, *The History of the Kings of Britain*, trans. Lewis Thorpe, Penguin, London, 1966, p. 181. The Cerne Abbas Giant lives on a hill in Dorset, England.

p. 23. Monmouth, *History of the Kings of Britain*, p. 168. According to Apuleius's *De deo Socratis*, incubi live between the earth and the moon.

p. 25. Robert de Boron, *Merlin and the Grail: Joseph of Arimathea, Merlin, Perceval: The Trilogy of Prose Romances Attributed to Robert de Boron*, trans. Nigel Bryant, D. S. Brewer, Woodbridge, 2001, p. 57.

Half-human, half-incubus, Baby Merlin defends his mother at her witch trial, while Boron must defend his own fascination with a pagan subject like Merlin.

p. 27. 'Owein, or the Countess of the Fountain', in *The Mabinogion*, p. 197. Gold or silver necklets in Celtic tales suggest that their wearers are fairy beasts.

p. 29. *Immram Brain: Bran's Journey to the Land of Women*, trans. Séamus Mac Mathúna, Max Niemeyer Verlag, Tübingen, 1985, p. 51. Golden sceptres and silver branches indicate the sovereignty of otherworldly deities; few mortals can wield such regalia.

p. 31. Laymon, *Brut*, quoted in Jeff Rider, 'The Fictional Margin: The Merlin of the Brut', *Modern Philology*, Vol. 87, No. 1, 1989, p. 8. Dragons are needed in contemporary poetry.

p. 33. Wace, *Arthurian Chronicles Represented by Wace and Layamon*, trans. Eugene Mason, J. M. Dent, London, 1912, p. 27. Celtic auguries were drawn from the flights and cries of birds.

p. 35. *The Prose Merlin*, trans. Samuel N. Rosenberg, in *The Romance of Arthur: An Anthology of Medieval Texts in Translation*, ed. James J. Wilhelm, Garland, London, 1994, p. 308. A fear of nature and the imagination was on the rise in twelfth-century Europe.

p. 37. *The Prose Merlin*, pp. 337–8.

p. 39. Wolfram von Eschenbach, *Parzival, with Titurel and the Love-lyrics*, trans. Julia Walworth, D. S. Brewer, Cambridge, 2004, p. 170. Here the Haughty Maiden of Logres chides our knight for his demonisation of the natural world.

p. 41. *The High Book of the Grail: A Translation of the Thirteenth-Century Romance of Perlesvaus*, trans. Nigel Bryant, D. S. Brewer, Ipswich, 1978, p. 162. Via sacred violence, destroyed weapons were sacrificed to the gods or neutralised in water.

p. 43. *Gods and Fighting Men*, p. 13. St Brigit was long preceded by Brigit, a Tuatha Dé Danann goddess worshipped both as crone and as spring maiden. The hooligan king is Dermot MacMurrough of Leinster.

p. 45. *The High Book of the Grail*, p. 77. Symbols of life, many Fisher Kings have appeared: Vishnu, Buddha, Tammuz, Christ, etc.

p. 47. *Alliterative Morte Arthure*, trans. Valerie Krishna, in *Romance of Arthur*, p. 508. In a dream prophesying the end of his empire, Lady Fortuna spins King Arthur to the bottom of her wheel.

p. 49. Thomas Malory, *Le Morte d'Arthur*, Modern Library, New York, 1999, p. 36. After unknowingly committing incest, Arthur sees a strange composite beast, symbolic of his empire's coming divisions and collapse.

p. 51. 'Peredur Son of Evrawg', p. 243. Peredur's marvellous flaming tree resonates with one that the Modernist H.D. experienced.

p. 53. 'Branwen Daughter of Llyr', p. 72. Canadian painter Emily Carr was haunted throughout her career by the image of the angry, powerful Kwakwaka'wakw ogress Dzunukwa.

p. 55. 'The Voyage of Maelduin', trans. Caitlín Matthews, in *The Celtic Book of the Dead*, St Martin's Press, New York, 1992, p. 20. God speaks out in Genesis 12:1 as again and again boats set sail for Avalon, Ys, Lyonesse, Atlantis, and the Isles of the Blessed.

Special thanks to Annie Beer, Vanessa Lodge, and Anushree Varma of the multi-talented Sednas; John Donlan, Kevan Manwaring, and Jay Ramsay for their exacting criticism and generosity of spirit; creativity coach Eric Maisel for his enthusiastic encouragement; and my husband and daughter, Spiro and Zoe Arniotis, for their patience and their inspired cooking.

www.awenpublications.co.uk

Also available from Awen Publications:

The Firekeeper's Daughter
Karola Renard

From the vastness of Stone Age Siberia to a minefield in today's Angola, from the black beaches of Iceland to the African savannah and a Jewish-German cemetery, Karola Renard tells thirteen mythic stories of initiation featuring twenty-first-century kelpies, sirens, and holy fools, a river of tears and a girl who dances on fire, a maiden shaman of ice, a witch in a secret garden, Queen Guinevere's magic mirror, and a woman who swallows the moon. The red thread running through them all is a deep faith in life and the need to find truth and meaning even in the greatest of ordeals.

'In her lively and vivid stories, Karola Renard points a finger towards the mythic threads that run through life's initiations.' *Martin Shaw*

Fiction ISBN 978-1-906900-46-5 £9.99

Crackle of Almonds: selected poems
Gabriel Bradford Millar

In these renegade poems ranging from 1958 to 2011 Gabriel Bradford Millar presents a spectrum of life, in all its piquant poignancy, with unfaltering precision, defiance, and finesse. From the very first to the very last, the breathtaking skill of this consummate wordsmith does not waver. Many of the poems linger in the air – not least because Millar performs them orally with such verve. She believes 'that poems, like love-talk, should go from mouth to ear without any paper in between'. On the page their orality and aurality fragrance their presence without diminishing their literary elegance. Continually astonishing, these epicurean poems not only offer a lasting testimony to a 'life well-lived', but inspire the reader to live well too

'She does not just write *about* the world; she dips her syllables in the bitter sweet of its "gazpacho". She thinks melodically.' *Paul Matthews*

Poetry ISBN 978-1-906900-29-8 £9.99

Soul of the Earth: the Awen anthology of eco-spiritual poetry
edited by Jay Ramsay

Beautifully crafted, yet challenging received wisdom and pushing boundaries, these are cutting-edge poems from a new generation of writers who share a love of the Earth and haven't given up on humans either. In poems as light as a butterfly and as wild as a storm you'll find vivid, contemporary voices that dare to explore a spiritual dimension to life on Earth and, in doing so, imply that a way out of our global crisis of ecological catastrophe, financial meltdown, and bankruptcy of the spirit is to look beyond the impasse of materialism. With contributions from poets in the USA, Canada, UK, Australia, and New Zealand, this anthology reaches out across the planet to embrace the challenges and blessings of being alive on the Earth in the twenty-first century.

'All real poetry seeks to "renew the face of the earth" – and so to resist the exploiting, banalization or defacing of what lies around us. I hope this collection will serve the renewal of vision we so badly need.'
Most Revd Dr Rowan Williams

Poetry ISBN 978-1-906900-17-5 £12.00

The Long Woman
Kevan Manwaring

An antiquarian's widow discovers her husband's lost journals and sets out on a journey of remembrance across 1920s England and France, retracing his steps in search of healing and independence. Along alignments of place and memory she meets mystic Dion Fortune, ley-line pioneer Alfred Watkins, and a Sir Arthur Conan Doyle obsessed with the Cottingley Fairies. From Glastonbury to Carnac, she visits the ancient sites that obsessed her husband and, tested by both earthly and unearthly forces, she discovers a power within herself.

'A beautiful book, filled with the quiet of dawn, and the first cool breaths of new life, it reveals how the poignance of real humanity is ever sprinkled with magic.' *Emma Restall Orr*

Fiction ISBN 978-1-906900-44-1 £9.99
The Windsmith Elegy Volume 1

Words of Re-enchantment: writings on storytelling, myth, and ecological desire

Anthony Nanson

The time-honoured art of storytelling – ancestor of all narrative media – is finding new pathways of relevance in education, consciousness-raising, and the journey of transformation. Storytellers are reinterpreting ancient myths and communicating the new stories we need in our challenging times. This book brings together the best of Anthony Nanson's incisive writings about the ways that story can re-enchant our lives and the world we live in. Grounded in his practice as a storyteller, the essays range from the myths of Arthur, Arcadia, and the voyage west, to true tales of the past, science-fiction visions of the future, and the big questions of politics and spirituality such stories raise. The book contains full texts of exemplar stories and will stimulate the thinking of anyone interested in storytelling or in the use of myth in fiction and film.

'This excellent book is written with a storyteller's cadence and understanding of language. Passionate, fascinating and wise.'
Hamish Fyfe

Storytelling/Mythology/Environment ISBN 978-1-906900-15-1 £9.99

Mysteries

Chrissy Derbyshire

This enchanting and exquisitely crafted collection by Chrissy Derbyshire will whet your appetite for more from this budding wordsmith. Her short stories interlaced with poems depict chimeras, femmes fatales, mountebanks, absinthe addicts, changelings, derelict warlocks and persons foolhardy enough to stray into the beguiling world of Faerie. Let the sirens' song seduce you into the Underworld.

'All of the pieces in *Mysteries* are entertaining. But they also speak twice. Each one has layers of meaning that touch on the ultimate that cannot be put into words and speak to our inner landscapes that are so full of desire for meaning.' *Kim Huggens*

Fiction/Poetry ISBN 978-1-906900-45-8 £8.99

Iona
Mary Palmer

What do you do when you are torn apart by your 'selves'? The pilgrim poet, rebel Mordec and tweedy Aelia set sail for Iona – a thin place, an island on the edge. It's a journey between worlds, back to the roots of their culture. On the Height of Storm they relive a Viking massacre, at Port of the Coracle encounter vipers. They meet Morrighan, a bloodthirsty goddess, and Abbot Dominic with his concubine nuns. There are omens, chants, curses ... During her stay Mordec learns that words can heal or destroy, and the poet writes her way out of darkness. A powerful story, celebrating a journey to wholeness, from an accomplished poet.

'Always truthful, this poetry confronts both beauty and ugliness and makes space for light to slip between the two.' *Rose Flint*

Poetry ISBN 978-0-9546137-8-5 £6.99
Spirit of Place Volume 1

A Dance with Hermes
Lindsay Clarke

In a verse sequence that swoops between wit and ancient wisdom, between the mystical and the mischievous, award-winning novelist Lindsay Clarke elucidates the trickster nature of Hermes, the messenger god of imagination, language, dreams, travel, theft, tweets, and trading floors, who is also the presiding deity of alchemy and the guide of souls into the otherworld. Taking a fresh look at some classical myths, this vivacious dance with Hermes choreographs ways in which, as an archetype of the poetic basis of mind, the sometimes disreputable god remains as provocative as ever in a world that worries – among other things – about losing its iPhone, what happens after death, online scams, and the perplexing condition of its soul.

'Lindsay Clarke's poems wonderfully embody what they describe: the god Hermes, who is comprehensively shown to be just as revelatory and double-dealing in the digital age as he ever was in antiquity.' *Patrick Harpur*

Poetry/Mythology ISBN 978-1906900-43-4 £10.00

Printed in Great Britain
by Amazon

36765492R00047